God's People at Worship

Story

A way of preaching in all-age worship

Michael J Townsend

Jointly published by
Division of Education and Youth
and
Methodist Publishing House

First published September 1991

ISBN 7192 0183 7
ISBN 0 946550 69 7

Illustrations: Helen Mahood

Jointly published by
Methodist Church Division of Education and Youth
2 Chester House, Pages Lane, London N10 1PR
and
Methodist Publishing House
20 Ivatt Way, Peterborough PE3 7PG

Printed by
Swannack Brown & Co Ltd,
13 Anlaby Road, Hull HU1 2PJ

God's People at Worship

An introduction to the series

'God's People at Worship' is a series of booklets about Christian worship, particularly as it takes place when all ages are present.

For simplicity, the phrase *all-age worship* is used throughout the series, despite its shortcomings. The word *worship* should need no qualification. In worship, people offer themselves – with all their similarities and differences (including their ages) – to God. Unfortunately, *worship* has come to be seen as a mainly adult activity. To describe it as *all-age* provides a useful reminder that it is the business of the whole people of God.

The booklets in the series deal with different aspects of all-age worship. In general, the emphasis is practical, looking at *How?* questions. However, *Why?* questions are also dealt with, particularly in the introductory volume, *One*.

'God's People at Worship' is for worship leaders; for those who plan, prepare and co-ordinate worship in local churches; for workers with children and young people; for church musicians; for people who are creative in written or spoken word, dance, drama or visual arts; for stewards, members of worship consultations and Church Councils and all those who make decisions about the church's worship. But above all, our hope is that these booklets will

be read and used by Christian people of all ages who care about worship.

This volume, *Story*, is mainly (but not exclusively) for preachers. It explores new and exciting possibilities for developing the Ministry of the Word in all-age worship through the use of story-sermons – a *creative and helpful way of commending the Good News*. Here is a way of bringing new freshness to familiar biblical material in presenting the Christian gospel to young and old alike.

'God's People at Worship' is produced jointly by the Methodist Publishing House and the Division of Education and Youth, in consultation with representatives of the Division of Ministries and the Worship Commission.

The General Editor of the series is Rev. David Gamble, working with an Advisory Group (Mrs Judy Jarvis, Rev. John Lampard, Mr Brian Sharp and Mr Brian Thornton).

Contents

A word to the reader

This is not a book to be read just once. Rather it is to be re-read, thought about and tried out in practice. At the end of each chapter there are suggestions *for further thought and action*. Hopefully, they will help you to develop on what is presented here.

1 Why story?

The word *story* conjures up a variety of associations in our minds. We sometimes say, *'Everyone has a story to tell'*, meaning that we find other people's life experiences interesting and moving. *'Tell me your story'* is something we might say to a person in need or trouble, knowing that by doing so they will be encouraged to unburden themselves and find help. Or we might comment, after watching a disappointing film or play, *'I didn't think much of the story-line'*. That remark tells us (if we didn't know it already) that a good story is one of the things we expect from our choice of entertainment.

Yet we are also aware that the best stories are never *merely* entertainment. We might not find it easy to define what the *'extra'* is, but we know it when it comes our way. The great stories of the world are those which teach us something about ourselves and about life. They speak powerfully about how human beings behave and interact and what we expect from life. Not infrequently, they introduce us to the notion of rewards and punishments, and they both reinforce and challenge moral codes. *Their greatest strength is that we scarcely realize they are doing these things!* Such a description might make them sound formidable, or at least excruciatingly dull, but, of course, they are nothing of the sort. If they were either of those things they would not have remained popular, to be read and re-told over and over again.

For much of our century, in industrial and technological societies at least, there has been a tendency to denigrate story-telling. Stories have often been seen as opposed to facts, and different from them. Some of the more negative associations the word story produces in our minds can be seen when we say to children *'Don't tell stories'*, by which we mean *'Don't tell untruths'*. Or we might remark to someone who has just related a rather implausible happening, *'That's a good story'*, meaning *'I don't believe a word of it really'*.

Charles Dickens, himself one of the finest of all story-tellers in English, satirized this attitude in his novel *Hard Times* in the person of the utilitarian schoolmaster Thomas Gradgrind who both ran his school and brought up his five children on the principle that only facts counted.

> No little Gradgrind had ever associated a cow in a field with that famous cow with the crumpled horn who tossed the dog who worried the cat who killed the rat who ate the malt, or with that yet more famous cow who swallowed Tom Thumb: it had never heard of those celebrities, and had only been introduced to a cow as a graminivorous ruminating quadruped with several stomachs.

Mr Gradgrind was wrong, of course. Story and narrative, art and imagination, are not opposed to factual reality, they are other ways of exploring reality. Because they draw on our imagination and call forth emotional responses they can be powerful ways of interpreting experience, the world – and God. To object that there never *was* a poor little girl called Cinderella who had ugly step-sisters would be to miss the point entirely, and we know it. In the same way, to insist that there never was a historical sower who went forth to sow and whose seed fell into four contrasted types of soil would be to misunderstand the whole point of the story Jesus told (Mark 4.3-9). We need stories, provided they are good ones, because they are an important part of being human.

> *Take a few moments to reflect on the stories you most enjoyed when you were a child. Why did you enjoy them, and what do you think you learned from them?*

When Jesus had something important to tell people about how God's kingdom works, he quite often told a story. We call them parables and there are almost thirty of them in the gospels. Some of them are quite long (the story of the Prodigal Son in Luke 15.11-32 is an example), whilst others occupy no more than a couple of verses (the Two Housebuilders in Luke 6.48-49 or the Parable of the Yeast, Luke 13.20-21). Some are answers to questions people asked, others are warnings to certain groups of people, and yet others seem to form part of planned teaching on the part of Jesus.

It is surely significant that when a religious lawyer asked Jesus a perfectly serious question about who should be defined as the *'neighbour'* he was commanded to love (Luke 10.29), Jesus chose to answer him with one of his best-known stories, about a *'good Samaritan'*. Jesus *could* have given him a formal definition of a neighbour, and the lawyer would have understood that. Instead, he told a story which still has the power to move and challenge us today. This provides *us* with all the justification we need for using the medium of story in our communication of the Good News. If Jesus did not regard telling a story as frivolous or lightweight, neither should we.

If we are going to use stories as a preaching medium, we should take careful note of some of the characteristics of Jesus' parables and learn from them.

1 The stories Jesus told mostly arose from real life situations. They are about people in family life; about

daily occupations such as sowing, ploughing, doing the housework or making bread; they are about knocking on the door of friends' houses when in trouble, about giving parties and going to weddings. Jesus, in our rather hackneyed phrase, *'began where people are'*. We should try to do the same.

2 The stories of Jesus were often open-ended. He sometimes began a story by asking, *'What do you think?'* and quite often ended, *'If you have ears to hear, then hear'*. The stories demanded a response, but that response was to be supplied by those who heard them. His hearers had to work out exactly what the story meant for themselves. Jesus did not spoil his stories by adding at the end, *'Now the moral of this story is . . .'*, and neither should we. It is true that here and there in the gospels we do find an *'explanation'* appended to a parable, but most scholars believe that these were added by the gospel-writers, rather than coming from Jesus himself. That is too large a question to deal with here, but the existence of such explanations does not invalidate the argument about the essential open-endedness of the stories Jesus told.

3 On other occasions, when the circumstances warranted it, Jesus left his hearers in no doubt whatever what they had to do as a result of the story they have heard (see Luke 7.36-50 for a good example). They are stories which demand a verdict. You are not left in any doubt here that you should love God because your sins, which are great, stand forgiven. Another excellent example, from the Old Testament, is that of David and the prophet Nathan (see 2 Samuel 12.1-7).

Without looking them up, make a list of the first six parables of Jesus which come to your mind. Which of them is open-ended and which demand a verdict?

When we have brought together in our minds (and perhaps on paper too), some of the things about the parables and about the stories we recall from our childhood which we most enjoy, we are well on the way to knowing what kind of stories we might create as effective vehicles of proclaiming the good news.

For further thought and action

1 What makes a good story?

2 What are the advantages of leaving a story open-ended or of making its meaning quite clear and demanding a verdict? Is there room for both kinds of story in preaching?

3 Can a good story speak to all ages? If so, think of some stories that do so. What can we learn from them?

4 Find a book of your favourite short stories or a book a children's stories. Read one or two.

2 What kinds of stories?

If telling stories in worship has been out of fashion for a good many years (and it has!) this is only partly because some have thought them too unsophisticated for contemporary society. It is also because in the past such stories have all-too-often been used as entertainment for the children (and for the adults too, if we are honest). Rightly recognizing that this is both patronizing to the children and a debasing of Christian worship, we have then thrown out the baby with the bath-water. The best

response is not to abandon story-telling, but to be clear about why we are doing it and what kinds of stories may appropriately be used. In this booklet we shall explore in more detail two kinds of story. These may be described as:

1 *Personalized narrative*
This is a rather clumsy way of describing something very simple. Personalized narrative is a way of re-telling a story which is found in the Bible as if you were one of the participants in the original story.

2 *Parallel narrative*
This kind of preaching involves constructing a story which is quite independent of the biblical text as regards its details and story-line, but which aims to re-create the impact of the original biblical passage for a contemporary audience.

These rather brief descriptions (which will need some expansion later on) are sufficient to enable us to see that story-preaching must *always* be related to, indeed based upon, biblical material. It is intended to illuminate, expound and commend the biblical message in exactly the same way as any other kind of preaching. Accordingly, it demands from those who attempt it just as much hard work. Telling a story can never be a short-cut in producing a message for worship.

We are specifically concerned here, with stories in the context of all-age worship. It is in this context that they have very real advantages as well as some dangers. It has often been recognized that the chief difficulty in giving an address at all-age worship is precisely that it *is* all-age! A careful and measured exegesis of one of the more difficult passages of a Pauline letter may command the attention and interest of those of God's people who have been on their pilgrimage for a good many years, but it certainly will not do very much for the under 10s. On the other hand, targeting the material we deliver at the under 10s often

leads to the complaint (and it has to be admitted that it is frequently justified) that the more experienced sheep look up and are not fed. When all-age worship is aimed at a notional *'mean'* (usually somewhere around the older Brownies) it is not unknown for those at both ends of the spectrum to vote with their feet.

Story-preaching, although not a complete answer to this difficulty, has within it the potential to offer something to the whole range of age and experience (the two are not the same) within the congregation. When it is well-done it provides at least the possibility that everyone present can own it and find something helpful in it. This is partly because of the open-endedness which we saw to be important with the parables of Jesus. If those who hear the story are enabled to, as it were, provide their own conclusion, they can supply it at whatever level of intellectual understanding and spiritual maturity is theirs. Good stories operate at a number of different levels; that is part of their virtue and their longevity!

Think about what you have just read concerning the difficulty of the address at all-age worship. Do you agree with it? How, in your experience, have worship leaders and preachers tried to deal with these problems? Do you think they were successful?

Back now to the two kinds of story, personalized narrative and parallel narrative, we have already briefly outlined. Since they are both based upon biblical material (though in rather different ways), the question to tackle is: *How are we going to tell the story presented to us by the biblical passage?* This question is essentially the same whether we have chosen the passage for ourselves or had it presented to us through a lectionary or some other scheme of reading.

The answer is that we first have to work on the biblical material in exactly the same way as if we were going to preach a traditional sermon. Experienced preachers in particular, will know how to do this, but we need to refresh our memories on some of the salient points. One thing in particular may be different: some preachers have the habit of preaching on a particular biblical text. There is much to be said for this, not least because it fixes the scriptural message in the minds of our hearers. But, of course, most individual biblical texts are themselves summaries, or the culmination, of longer passages. If we are preaching on a single text we usually do that in the light of the larger passage of scripture of which it is part. In story-preaching, although it will not do any harm to have a single text as a summary, it will usually be found most helpful to preach on the passage *as a whole*.

Our next task is *exegesis*. We do not need to be afraid of this word; it merely means finding out what the text meant to those who wrote it and to those who first read, heard or experienced it. We think our way back into the minds of those to whom the message first came. What kind of

people were they? What were their worries, hopes, sins and achievements? Is there a background of customs, practices and assumptions against which the text must be read in order for us to correctly understand what it meant? What did the words used in the passage mean in their original language?

Fortunately, we have many things to help us here. If we do not know the answers to many of those questions (or even if we think we do!) a good commentary and a Bible dictionary will usually set us right and save us from making elementary mistakes. *The process of exegesis is about finding the centre-point of the passage.* It may surprise us to realize that once we have done this, and thought our way into its original meaning, we are a good way towards having the essential material for writing a story-sermon. In more conventional preaching the next stage would be *exposition*. We would take what we had understood about the original meaning and let it interact with our contemporary concerns and problems until the word of scripture for today's world came through. Or (since the above is by no means the only way to write sermons), if we had begun with some aspect of living Christianity in our times and looked to the Bible for illumination, exposition would be the point at which we saw how to interpret the one in the light of the other. However, instead of constructing an exposition with, say, three points, an introduction and conclusion and appropriate illustrations, we are going to write a story about it!

For further thought and action

1. Can you remember any stories that have made you stop and think, or stories through which you have learned something new?
2. Think of a non-biblical story you know which illustrates some biblical truth. Tell it aloud - either to yourself or to a friendly listener. How easy do you find story-telling?
3. If you had a listener, ask them to retell the story to you (and consider what this shows about your story-telling technique).
4. Try taping yourself telling a story. Then listen to the tape. What are your strengths and weaknesses as a story-teller?

3 How to write personalized narratives

Since an ounce of example is worth a pound of precept, we shall consider actual examples of the kinds of stories we might use in worship, with some questions concerning the things which worked, or did not work, for us.

We have already seen that *personalized narrative* is about re-telling the biblical story as if we had actually been a participant in it. Of course, whenever we tell a story – any kind of story – we interpret it in the telling. Interpretation is found in the weight we give to the various characters involved in the story, in the words we use to describe what happened, even in the tone of voice in which we tell it. The case is no different with story-sermons. This is where our exegesis comes in. We know that our telling of the story will be an interpreted telling, but we want that interpretation to be based on a sound understanding of the meaning of the original. Take, for example, the story of Zacchaeus (Luke 19.1-10). Our work on the text (aided by commentaries and dictionaries) will suggest the following considerations are important in understanding the meaning of the story.

> Tax-collectors were collaborators with the occupying Roman authorities and were therefore despised by orthodox religious people.

- Tax-collectors would not (unless they repented) be considered clean, and were thus unwelcome to participate in religious ceremonies.
- By going to stay at a 'sinner's' house Jesus caused great scandal.
- Zacchaeus was so moved by the action of Jesus that he repented, and showed his repentance by promising more restitution to his victims than the law strictly required.
- The final words of Jesus (Luke 19.10) are the heart of the story. It is by encountering Jesus that people are changed, and this is why he came.

Now we have to decide which character's viewpoint will shape our telling of the story. It would be too easy to be one of the bystanders, since the whole point of the story is about change brought about by an encounter with Jesus. Then why not tell it from Zacchaeus' point of view? After all, he was the person to whom exciting things happened! Of course, we have to engage in an imaginative exercise as well. We need to help our congregation understand what kind of a person Zacchaeus was, to feel that they know him. The very act of putting the background information into the first person makes it more vivid. Consider the contrast between these two passages:

The Romans did not pay their tax-collectors a proper wage. Instead they worked on a commission basis, allowing them to collect taxes from their district in their own way. Provided the agreed amount was handed over to the authorities the tax-collectors kept whatever else they managed to raise as their 'wages'. This was a clear incentive to greed.

You would think it might be easier if the Romans paid me a proper wage, wouldn't you? But they don't. I work on a commission basis. They tell me what taxes to produce from my district each year and anything I collect over and above that I keep for myself as pay. I make quite sure I do, too!

Here, then, is the result.

My name is Zacchaeus. I'm an ordinary sort of chap really; middle forties, starting to go bald on top, wife, three children - all the usual things. Actually, I've done rather well for myself. I wasn't much good at school and the family wondered what I was going to do in life. Father was a Parson, but I didn't fancy that - quite the opposite in fact. So I joined the civil service instead. Now, don't laugh. Civil servants are very necessary. We work very hard. Of course, I've done quite well out of it. I have a rather pleasing purpose-built villa in the suburbs of Jericho and an income that is adequate for most of our needs. No real grumbles, then.

What branch of the civil service, did you say? I thought you did. Well, actually, I'm a fiscal operative. Oh, all right - I'm

a tax-collector. There! I knew that would be the reaction; it always is. But let me tell you, being a tax-collector is a very responsible job. How else would the Government get its money? But yes, I know what you're thinking, and you are right. There *are* some problems. I know that no loyal Jew would ever think of becoming a tax-collector. Of course they would if we were collecting for our own Jewish government. It is because we are collecting for the Romans who are occupying our country that people object so strongly. A lot of our friends dropped me when I joined the service. They said it was disloyal to God and my fellow Israelites. Well, maybe; but with all this unemployment about you have to earn a living somehow. I admit I found the system a bit strange at first. I mean: you would think it would be a lot easier if the Romans paid me a proper wage. But they don't. I work on a kind of commission basis. They tell me what taxes to produce from my district each year, and anything I can collect over and above that I keep as my pay. I make sure I do too! I hope I haven't exactly ground the faces of the poor, but I've ground the faces of the rich a few times, and some of the moderately well-off in my district aren't as moderately well-off as they used to be.

I don't know that you would describe me as a very religious man. In a way I can't be. It was made very clear to me the day I became a tax-collector that I wouldn't be very welcome in church. I don't mind too much. I've always said that you can be just as good a Jew without ever going to church. In any case, most of the people who do go to church are hypocrites. But for some strange reason, I still enjoy going to religious meetings - the open-air sort that aren't held in church. It always gives me a big thrill to hear a really good preacher.

That is why, last week, when I heard that Jesus of Nazareth was coming to town, I got quite excited. He has a *real* reputation; those hypocritical Pharisees don't like him so he can't be all bad, I thought. A customer was telling me last week that he is the holiest man he has ever met. He said that when you met Jesus you knew you had met someone really good.

It was Thursday when he arrived, and I went out to see him. There was a terrific crowd everywhere. Oh, did I forget to mention - I'm a bit on the short side. When I got to the spot

where Jesus was coming along the road, I couldn't see anything. There was a great big fat man in front of me with a briefcase, and a woman with a child on her shoulders, and I didn't think I was going to be able to see Jesus at all. Then I had a bright idea. There was a tree just behind me, so I shinned up it and was head and shoulders above the rest of the crowd. Only just in time, too! Jesus was very near. He looked ordinary enough and I was just starting to wonder what all the fuss was about when, suddenly, it happened!

Jesus looked up. He looked straight at me, and he said, *'Zacchaeus, come down'*. I couldn't believe my ears, but he went on, 'Hurry, because I have to stay at your house today'. You should have *heard* the reaction of the crowd! Old Ben Eliazar whose taxes I had collected the previous day said several very rude things, and others said that if this Jesus was going to my house he couldn't be as holy as he made out to be!

None of that mattered to me. I simply knew, from the moment Jesus spoke to me that nothing was ever going to be the same again. For years, as a boy, I had listened to preachers telling me how to be good. My father hardly ever stopped telling me how to be good, it was one of his favourite subjects. And I'd tried, at least at one time. Then I would begin to think that perhaps it would do if I wasn't any worse than anyone else, or at least, not *much* worse, and so it went on. All the preaching in the world couldn't change me. But Jesus did. He didn't tell me how bad I'd been; quite the opposite. He seemed to accept me just as I was. There was something about his look and his words. When he spoke to me I suddenly felt for the first time in my life that I *wanted* to be good - and that I could be! I can't explain that, so don't ask me to try. It was meeting with Jesus which changed it all for me, and now there isn't anything that I wouldn't do for him.

I wanted to show that I understood what had happened, so I told him: *'If I have done anything wrong (and I knew I had), I will pay it back four times over'*. That wasn't an empty promise. I knew it was going to cost me a lot, and it has done. But every sacrifice that I have had to make - I'm still out of work now that I have resigned from the service - has been well worth it. Jesus said to me, *'Today salvation has come to this house, because this man too is a son of*

Abraham'. I knew that meant that God loved me. I had never really understood that before.

So all I can say, from my own experience is this. You can listen to all the good advice in the world. You can try to keep the rules as hard as ever you can. But it won't make you a really good person. If you meet with Jesus - I mean really meet with him, something will happen. You will actually begin to change. That is what has happened to me. I know I've got a long way to go, but at least I'm on the right path now. It is Jesus who has done that for me. I hope you will let him do it for you, as well.

That story-sermon was originally written for an adult, rather than all-age congregation. It has been allowed to stand unrevised in order that we may do our own thinking about how it might be adapted.

What do you think it presently offers to

a the under 5s

b teenagers

c those who have been coming to church for fifty years or more?

- *What changes would you like to make to it in order to make it more effective for each of these groups?*
- *Are those changes largely concerned with vocabulary, style or something else?*

Finally, on this one, an actual reaction to ponder. When that sermon was preached to an *'ordinary'* congregation in the West Midlands, a church steward commented in the vestry afterwards: *'That is exactly how my old Sunday School Superintendent used to tell the Bible stories, and they have lived with me ever since'.*

Personalized narrative is useful with lesser-known biblical stories, but it can also illuminate those which everybody knows well, but where we tend to draw the *'wrong'* conclusions. The story of David and Goliath is certainly well-known, but the danger of telling it when children are present is that it is almost *too* well-known! There is an assumption that the message of the story is that bullies get put in their place – and that is certainly an idea with which children can identify! Although that element is undoubtedly present in the biblical narrative, it is not the dominant theme. At one level this might not cause us too much worry. Stories, after all, are multi-layered, and hearers (adults as well as young people and children) will interpret them at the level of their own needs. Nevertheless, a preacher engaged in responsible exegesis will want to ensure that the overall thrust of the way the story is told does not mislead by presenting one strand of the biblical narrative as though it were *the* message we should derive from the passage.

Space does not permit here a detailed exegesis of 1 Samuel 17. 1- 51. Suffice it to say that the *centre-point of the passage* is found in verse 47: *'. . . and everyone here will see that the Lord does not need swords or spears to save his people'.* The story of David and Goliath is centrally concerned with Israel's belief that their God was mighty to save (in every sense), even against the odds. In writing a personalized story-sermon based on this well-known narrative, therefore, the contrast needs to be drawn between reliance on your own strength (which is foolish) and reliance on God's strength (which is much wiser).

To tell the story from David's point of view might put us in danger of moralism. It is also likely to evoke a fairly speedy reaction from younger listeners something along the lines of: *'We know the ending of this – the goody will win'. The preacher's task of making goodness interesting is not made easy when the outcome of the story is already known.* There is no way of evading that difficulty, but it can be minimized by telling the story from Goliath's point of view. He, after all, is the obvious strong *'hero'* figure, with which many children will first identify. In choosing to do this, we have to consider carefully how to flesh out the figure of Goliath as he appears in the biblical text. We actually know very little about him, especially when set alongside the large amount of information available on David. The following example of how it might be done takes huge leaps of imagination in fleshing out the figure of Goliath and in presenting him as all brawn and no brain. If the historical Goliath was really a sensitive and cultured individual then, of course, we do him an injustice; but the risk seems worth taking!

In this particular version also, the preacher *steps back* one pace from the narrative, by presenting it as a document which has come into his or her hands. The advantages or disadvantages of doing this might profitably be pondered, but this is the result:

Into my possession a few weeks ago, came a very strange document. It was written in the ancient Philistine language, a little like Hebrew and a little like Ancient Egyptian. Though there are words missing here and there it is reasonably complete up to the point where it ends, somewhat abruptly. It tells an interesting story, and I have had it translated. I think the best thing I can do is to read it to you now. It is called, Goliath of Gath - my story.

I Goliath, champion of the Philistine people, am taking advantage of a few hours free before this evening's battle to write these notes. It was a great surprise when the publishers Albatross Books of Ashkelon asked me to write a book about myself. I am not very good at writing and I will ask my brother, who is better, to help me. The publishers say it will be a big seller. Everybody in our main towns, Gath, Ashkelon, Gaza, Ashdod and Ekron will be buying copies and I will be very rich. I am already famous. Today I am just making these few notes about my interesting life. When I have time I will write it into a proper book.

I Goliath, was born in Gath eighteen years ago. I don't remember much about my mother. She was always having children. In any case, she was a weak and stupid woman. My father always says not to take any notice of women - they don't know anything. I was a big baby, so my father says. I remember that when I was only three years old I was already a metre tall. My father was very proud of me. Even then I was bigger than my brother, who is older - and stronger, too. Once a cousin of mine came to see me and play for the afternoon, but I didn't want to play silly children's games. When he said something bad to me I hit him very hard and he cried a lot. My mother said that was bad, but my father said that it was good to be strong like that.

When I was five I had to go to school. Some things I liked about school and some things I didn't. We had prayers at school. That was strange because my father wouldn't let us have prayers at home. He said that prayers were only for women. But at school we said prayers to a god called Dagon. I used to ask Dagon to make me even bigger and stronger. I was very pleased because my prayers worked.

By the time I was eight I was nearly one and a half metres tall. My father was even prouder of me then. Some of the things I didn't like about school was learning things. I wasn't very good at that. I hated reading and history and religion and things like that. The only thing I really liked was games. Because I was much bigger and stronger than all the other boys, I could always win with any game I played.

We had a really horrible teacher. He was always trying to make us learn things I didn't want to. Once at the end of term, he wrote something on my report which made my father very angry. He wrote: *'Goliath is strong in the arm and thick in the head'*. When my father saw it he went straight round to the school to see the teacher and he . . . (here a word or two is missing from the text).

Before I left school, I formed my own gang. I was leader, of course. We used to go out in the evening Israelite-bashing. Some of those Israelites used to live in Gath and if we caught one we used to beat him up. My father said that Dagon would be pleased, but by that time I didn't believe in Dagon any longer. I know everyone said he was a great god, even greater than Ashtaroth, but I didn't need him any longer. At sixteen I was nearly two and a half metres tall and I could manage for myself. It is only weaklings and women who need a god. That's what I think, anyway.

I went in for one or two competitions - things like weight-lifting. I always won because I was the strongest. I've got a medal at home. It says on it: *'Goliath of Gath - Strongest of the Philistines'*. My father is in the army. We've got a good army, we Philistines. So when I got away from school I went into the army too. The assault courses and things like that were great. I really learned in the army what my father always said was true; if you were strong enough you can get anything you want. Strong? I was so big and strong that the army has had to have a special suit of armour made for me. None of the reg (this word has been altered once or twice, but I think it is *'regulation'*) armour would fit me. They made me a special set of bronze armour, real heavy. In no time at all I became what they call the *'Champion'* of the Philistine army.

That's why I must stop writing in half a tick. We've got something very big on tonight. A few days ago we started a war against these Israelites. Our army set off, and we camped at a place called Ephes-dammim. The Israelites have got their silly little army on the hills at the other side, but there aren't very many of them so we could beat them easy. We may not fight at all - except for me, of course. The two Generals have agreed on what they call a *'Champions Fight'*. That means the champion of *their* army against the champion of *ours*. Whoever wins that, their side will win the war.

I shouted the challenge across the valley and they all looked very scared of me (people usually are). For a while there was no answer, but then a little later, there was. The Israelites have got a champion to take me on. *'Take me on'!* That's a laugh. I've seen him; he's no more than a boy. I shouldn't think he's started shaving yet. And he hadn't any proper armour with him. They must be stupid to think that anyone is bigger and stronger than Goliath. Anyway, the battle is on for tonight. Later on I shall have yet another trophy to put with all the others. I'll teach these stupid Israelites a lesson. One of our spies came back and said that this boy champion of theirs was busy saying his prayers to his god! Well he might! I don't need to say any prayers anymore. I'm not weak like he is. The only time I talk about Dagon is when I want to swear.

Anyway enough for now. I must go and put my armour on. Then I'll go and deal with this young Israelite. That will teach them you've got to be strong to succeed. Saying your prayers won't help. You've got to rely on your *own* strength. When I come back, I'll write some more about me, so everyone will read it and know how big and strong Goliath is.

Postscript At this point the manuscript breaks off abruptly, and there isn't any more of it. Fortunately, of course, we do have a supplementary source: (Read 1 Samuel 17. 37-51).

That story-sermon (unlike the previous example) *was* written for an all-age congregation. Again, ask yourself:

- *At what level and in what way it might have been understood by different age-groups within the congregation?*
- *How do you react to the obvious exercise of imagination in describing the character of Goliath?*
- *What is the borderline between fleshing out a character and parodying that same character, and is that borderline over-stepped in this example?*

It is an interesting reflection that the sermon was subsequently preached, entirely unaltered, to an evening all-adult congregation which included some students in higher education. They made their appreciation very clear,

as did Kevin. Kevin is a mentally-retarded adult who quite often comes to evening worship. He frequently leaves before, or during the sermon, and on the occasions when he does not, he passes the time by doing other things than listening (sometimes audibly doing other things!). He listened to that story-sermon all the way through, and on the way out commented with the rather perceptive response: *'I liked that story. Goliath was very silly. He should have said his prayers to God'.*

This is, perhaps, the point at which to reflect on the reaction of congregations in general to story-sermons, both in all-age worship and on other occasions. The responses I have received have helped to shape my understanding of what I am doing when I preach in this way.

Often, after a story-sermon has been used in worship, the people who normally do not react verbally to more standard sermons, ask questions, show interest and make comments. Some (though not all) of those who can usually be relied upon to make some kind of response to what has been said leave church with no more than a polite *'good-morning'* and just occasionally one of those will say, *'I'm afraid that didn't do anything for me today'*. The children and young people have not often reacted immediately. although when they have, it has been the form of wanting to add *'their bit'* to the story – especially from the younger children.

Where the response amongst the younger members of the congregation can be judged is by the fact that they generally listen! Perhaps that is reward enough. So far as the adults are concerned, it is reasonable to conclude that there are those in churches who, whilst accepting that sermons are a part of worship and no doubt receiving something from them from time to time, do not naturally think in the conceptual categories we often employ in our preaching. These are the ones who say nothing to the preacher at the door. But experience suggests that they *will* often say something when they have heard a story-sermon. Preaching in stories at all-age worship therefore, not only stands a chance of reaching the children and young people, but also of appealing to adults who most naturally approach life in that kind of way. Thus it is truly an *all*-age method and not just for the younger people present.

For further thought and action

1 How did you react to the stories in this chapter?

2 Would they be sufficient as a sermon in an act of worship or would more need to be said?

3 Retell the story of the Prodigal Son (Luke 15.11-32) from the point of view of the older brother.

4 If you feel more adventurous, try writing a last letter home from one of the prophets of Baal, explaining to his mum what happened in 1 Kings 18.

4 How to write parallel narratives

As has already been said, parallel narrative involves constructing a story which is quite independent of the biblical text as regards its details and story-line, but which aims to re-create the impact of the original biblical passage for a contemporary audience. That idea needs a little more exploration.

We have already been reminded in chapter two of the necessity to undertake our exegesis before beginning work on a story-sermon. If nothing else, this is because otherwise telling a story could become an easy option, and if challenged to show that the story we had told was properly grounded in the truths to be found in the scriptures we would be unable to do it. Such story-telling would not be responsible, nor indeed would it be preaching.

Having done our exegetical work to the best of our ability, and thus assembled the raw materials, we once again need to ask where the main thrust of the biblical passage lies. Unlike a conventional sermon, which may have several points, a story-sermon will usually have one, or at least, only one which *we* intended. In this too, they will be like the parables of Jesus. For example, if the lectionary reading is Galations 3.1-14 and the act of worship at which we are expected to deal with it is all-age worship, we might well quail inwardly! Paul at his most vigorous in dealing with the nature of justification is fairly strong meat for seasoned church-goers. For the children and the young in faith it is likely to be entirely incomprehensible, however simply we try to explain it. What, however, if our reading and re-reading of the passage convinces us that the main thrust is found not so much in any particular verse as in a summary which might run: *'We do not enter into a right relationship with God by keeping the rules, but by responding to his love'?* Granted that such a summary does not encompass everything in the passage (how could it?), can something be done with that by means of a story-sermon? It might be possible, for example, to tell a story of a woman who foolishly thought that the way to gain and hold the love of her husband and children was by always keeping rules and never being in the wrong. As time went on it became obvious to everyone but her that she was turning into a rather unpleasant person. Only when something happened in her life which involved her in having to admit she was in the wrong did it finally dawn on her that her family loved her no matter what she did. From that moment she was released from the grip of her own efforts at making herself lovable, to become a much more whole person.

Parallel narratives generally work better with adults than they do with children, and are therefore less suitable for all-age worship. The reason for this is that often a parallel narrative has to draw on experience of the adult world which the children do not share. Also, one of the reasons why story-sermons often succeed in re-creating the impact of the original biblical material is because the biblical material is well-known and the end of the story is therefore predictable. Children, on the whole, do not know the biblical material as well as that, and the need to rescue it from staleness is not present in the same way. Indeed, the use of personalized narrative can help to introduce children to biblical material with which they are unfamiliar in a fairly painless way. Nevertheless, there are still occasions when a parallel narrative might well be used. This is especially so if the amount of background explanation required to make the actual biblical narrative intelligible to young people is likely to create boredom or impatience along the way.

The first story-sermon I ever wrote concerned a certain Alderman Blenkinsopp and his grandson Thomas. It was written for an all-adult congregation (for Ash Wednesday) and has never been preached in the context of all-age worship. Indeed, it would be quite unsuitable for such an occasion. However, it seemed worth trying to re-tell the story from the point of view of the grandson Thomas, rather than the perspective of a detached narrator as in the original. Since space only permits the inclusion of one example of a parallel narrative story-sermon, it is the all-age worship version which is given here. Those who might be interested in comparing it with the rather different original will find that in *Worship and Preaching*, vol.12 no. 5, October 1982, pp. 5-7.

This is the story of Tom and his grandfather. Ever since he could remember, Tom had disliked his grandfather. That might seem a terrible thing to say but it was true. When he was very small Tom used to go to tea at his grandfather's house on Sundays, and it was always an awful experience. Grandfather's favourite word seemed to be *'Don't'*. He began many of his sentences with it: *'Don't talk with your mouth full, Thomas'; 'Don't argue with your grandmother, Thomas'; 'Don't tease the dog, Thomas'* - and a good many more besides.

Thomas quite liked his grandmother. She was little and very quiet, but she had a lovely smile. That was more than could be said for grandfather. He seemed very old to Tom, even then, with a bushy white moustache and a somewhat gruff voice. He talked all the time in short sharp sentences, as if he were giving orders - and indeed, he often was! When Tom went to tea on Sunday he was not allowed to do anything he enjoyed. There were no toys to be played with, and the television was never switched on. Sometimes, if the weather was fine they would go for a short walk, but most of the time Tom just had to sit and listen to grandfather talk. He could read, if he really wanted to, but grandfather would always inspect the book he had brought with him, and Tom could only read it if grandfather approved of it. Grandfather didn't seem to approve of many books, and only those about people in the Bible were really certain to be allowed.

Once, Tom has asked if he could bring one of his friends with him and, to his surprise, grandfather had said he could. But that wasn't a success either. Tom's friend was so bored he said he would never go again, and that was just as well because grandfather found out that the boy's parents didn't go to church, and told Tom that he was bad company for him.

Grandfather, you see, was religious. He was also very rich, and quite well-known in the town where he lived. Sometimes people would say to Tom: *'Aren't you lucky, having Mr Blenkinsopp for your grandfather?'* Tom, who didn't think he was lucky at all, would keep quiet! Grandfather was something called an *'Alderman'*. When Tom was young he didn't know exactly what that was, only that people thought it was something very important. It was only when he grew up that he learned it was someone who had served on the town council for a very long time and was considered important in the life of the community. Tom *did* know that grandfather was very rich. He lived in a very big house and had someone to drive him about in a very big car, so there was no doubt about that. Tom knew, too, that grandfather was very religious. On Sunday mornings they all went to church together (only grandfather called it *'chapel'*). It was called Bethesda, and they had their own special seats there; grandfather and grandmother, Tom's mother and father and his sister, Jane. Grandfather was very important in the life of the chapel as well. It was known that quite a lot of his money had been put into building it in the first place, and he also paid for a lot of things that needed doing. The minister was always very polite to grandfather and always asked him what he thought about things.

In Tom's mind, grandfather's money and grandfather's religion somehow went together. That's not surprising really, because grandfather used to talk to him quite a lot on those dreary Sunday afternoons, about how Tom could be a success in life. *'Now you mark my words young Thomas'*, he would say, *'it says in the Bible: "Blessed is the man that feareth the Lord, that delighteth greatly in his commandments . . . wealth and riches shall be in his house and his righteousness endureth for ever"'*. That was Alderman Blenkinsopp's favourite bit from the Bible. He taught young Tom that if you gave God the duty you owed him, and kept all his rules in the Bible, he would look after you.

All that was quite a long time ago because, as he grew up, Tom began to drift away from his grandfather and his grandfather's house. And he also, I'm sorry to say, began to drift away from Bethesda chapel as well – it reminded him too much of grandfather. When he was young, he had to do as he was told, however much he disliked it, but as he became older he started to protest: *'Mum, do I have to go to grandfather's today?'* he would plead. And of course, the day came when he didn't have to go to grandfather's and he never did, ever again.

In fact, when Tom left school I am afraid things didn't go very well for him. Grandfather would no doubt have given him a very good job in the big factory he owned if Tom had behaved differently towards him, but it was too late to change that. So though he found himself his own flat, where he could do what he liked, he had only a very poorly-paid job. Some of the escapades he got up to were just a bit silly, like most young lads do, and there was no harm in them.

Others were not so innocent, and I am sorry to have to tell you that it was only a year or so after he left school that he got into real trouble. He did something very silly - and very wrong. Because it was his first offence he was put on probation; otherwise he might easily have gone to prison. But, of course, he lost his job, so life became very miserable indeed. Grandfather by this time wanted nothing to do with him and had sent a message that he was never again to enter the house, so there was no help to be expected from that quarter. His parents would have liked to have helped, but they were afraid of grandfather and though they made sympathetic noises, nothing was done.

One evening, sitting in his flat, Tom began to wonder what was going to happen to his life. There didn't seem to be any point to it somehow, and there certainly was not much fun. He began to think of a girl he had met in the coffee-bar that morning. He had never seen her before, but she was sort of all lit-up from inside. She had a kind of glow. Tom, who liked chatting to pretty girls, had tried to get into conversation with her. After a few minutes, to his great surprise, she had invited him to a meeting that evening in her local church. She explained, *'I'm a Christian'*. *'A Christian!'* said Tom, *'Why, my grandfather reckons he's a Christian, and he's the most miserable self-righteous old prig anyone ever met'*. The girl just smiled and said *'Christians aren't really like that. Just remember, God loves you and Jesus died for you'* - and with that she was gone. Tom dismissed the conversation from his mind. He'd had quite enough of chapel, thank you! But that evening, wondering what was going to happen to his life, what the girl had said came back to him. He remembered how happy and friendly she had been, and he wanted to be like that. So, to his own very great surprise, he decided to say his prayers.

By a curious coincidence, at exactly the same moment, on the other side of town, Alderman Blenkinsopp lay dying. All the family (except Tom) were gathered round the bedside. The old man's voice was weak, but firm: *'All my life I've done my duty to God. I have feared the Lord. I have never wronged anyone, nor have I ever done a mean thing. You know that, I know that and God knows that. As the Bible says of such people, "wealth and riches shall be in his house". I have nothing to fear'*. And with that, the old man went to his Maker.

Thus it was that God found himself listening to two prayers at the same moment - he's quite used to that! One was grandfather's prayer, the other was Tom's prayer, and it went like this: *'Lord, I have done wrong, help me and save me'*.

Two men went up to the Temple to pray, one a Pharisee, the other a tax-collector. The Pharisee stood up and said this prayer to himself: *'I thank you, God, that I am not grasping, unjust, adulterous like the rest of mankind, and particularly that I am not like this tax-collector here. I fast twice a week; I pay tithes on all I get'*. The tax-collector stood some distance away, not even daring to raise his eyes to heaven; but he beat his breast and said: *'God be merciful to me, a sinner'*. This man, I tell you went home again at rights with God; the other did not. (Luke 18.9-14)

God reads the heart, not the obituaries. We all stand in need of mercy and grace. In Christ we are offered it. Thanks be to God.

The techniques used in creating that particular story-sermon were simple enough. They involved fitting contemporary equivalents for Pharisees and tax-collectors and developing a story-line which allowed the two attitudes to come into contact and contrast with each other in such a way that the issues can be seen. The capacity to work out a story-line cannot really be taught, but anyone who has told bed-time stories to their children will not find it difficult, and it involves little more than the exercise of a disciplined imagination. The only way to find out if you can do it is to keep practising until it begins to come more easily.

The questions which might legitimately be asked about the above example are many.

- *At what level might the very young children have understood it?*
- *Is there a danger that some of the adults will think you are simply being rude about 'chapel culture' and will they resent the identification of a senior chapel figure with Pharisaism?*
- *If they do, is that a bad thing, or does it, perhaps, raise the kinds of questions in our minds which the parable Jesus told would have raised in the minds of the first hearers?*

One thing which may have appeared odd, is that the scripture lesson was read after, indeed immediately after, the sermon, rather than before it, as is usually the case. The reason for this is that if the scripture reading precedes the sermon there is a danger that some of the adults in particular will spend a good part of the time when they should be listening to the sermon working out *how* the story parallels what they have just heard. Of course there is no way of guaranteeing that, once people realize you are embarked on a story-sermon they will not spend time trying to work out which passage of scripture you are going to read at the end! But that is a much more difficult thing to do. In the above example, for instance, it would not be very evident that Luke 18.9-14 was the chosen passage until very near the end. Indeed, some might have reached the conclusion by half-way through that it was going to be the story of the prodigal son!

It is worth asking the question whether the scripture passage always needs to be read. It is impossible to be dogmatic about this, but in general it is advisable to do so. This is partly in order that people may hear and understand that the story-sermon is not a fanciful invention but a genuine exposition of a biblical truth, and partly because we must never give the impression that stories *we* tell have some sort of theological or liturgical priority over the biblical word. What we do ought to be clearly seen to be derivative from and dependent upon, scripture.

Just occasionally after preaching a parallel narrative story-sermon, the preacher will be asked: *'Did that really happen?'* The wise answer will be: *'Does that matter?'*

For further thought and action

1 Could you describe to someone else the difference between a personalized narrative and a parallel narrative?

2 Are there situations in which one is clearly preferable to the other?

3 What does it mean to suggest that a story is "true" even though it didn't really happen?

4 Try writing a parallel narrative to be completed by reading Luke 9.57-62.

5 Do the same for Matthew 13.44. Try this as a children's story, then as a story for an adult congregation. What's the difference? Does there need to be a difference?

5 Techniques of story-telling

One of the questions traditionally asked at trial services conducted by preachers *'On Trial'* is: *Was the preacher tied to his/her notes?* The implication is that to be so tied to your notes is a bad thing. Indeed it is, though some quite magnificent preachers have been extremely dependent on the script in front of them. Story-sermons offer the possibility of a preacher using several different techniques, each with their own validity.

Most stories, especially parallel narrative ones, ought to give the impression of spontaneity, and of familiarity in the sense that the congregation feel it is a story that the teller knows well. If we can, therefore, it is usually good to memorize and absorb the main outlines and tell it as naturally as we can, whether we have a full script, brief notes, or headings in front of us. There is also, however, a very acceptable tradition of *reading* stories; this is something with which many children will be familiar. Public libraries often organize story-reading sessions on Saturdays or in school holidays, and children may have stories read to them at home (with increasing familiarity resulting in their strong objection being voiced when the reader changes anything!). If the story lends itself to this, therefore, deliberately and visibly reading from the script can be quite effective. The personalized story-sermon on Goliath and David would be one such, because it purports to be a manuscript which has come into the preacher's possession. Trial and error will be the best guide here.

It is certainly worth reading and hearing how other people tell stories. Visit your local library and look at a variety of story books. Listen to stories told on radio or television. Observe a school-teacher or parent telling or reading a story to children. Notice ways in which attention is held. Are questions sometimes asked to allow people to contribute to the telling of the story?

It is also worth considering points like where you should stand (or sit?) to tell your story. Is the pulpit the best or only place? And is the congregation well-placed for listening to a story? Might this be an occasion to invite them to come closer?

Some people are natural story-tellers. Others have to work hard to develop the techniques. But, even if it is hard work, the effort is repaid and well worth while.

For further thought and action

1. How do you react to all you have read in this book?
2. What can you do now which will help you try out some of what you have read? (It may be safest to start with a simple re-telling of a well-known biblical story from a different point of view.) When will you do it?

6 Limitations

All that has been said so far is a commendation of story-preaching and an exploration of some of its possibilities. It would be unwise to assume, though, there are no difficulties and problems. In his excellent book *Communicating Conviction* (Epworth Press, London 1983), Peter Brooks singles out two. The first is that the story does not always communicate the conviction intended by the story-teller, and it can delude both hearers and teller into thinking that much has been communicated when in fact very little has. We may respond to the first difficulty by saying that to be aware of it is to be a good way towards the solution. If the exegesis has been thoroughly done first, and we are as clear as we can possibly be in our own minds what it is we intend to communicate, then the risk is no greater than it is with a conventional sermon and we have to be content to leave the Holy Spirit to do His work.

The second problem is that stories relate to truth and communicate their messages in different ways. If then, the story-teller is working in one idiom, and the hearers in another, what is communicated may be false or even harmful. Peter Brooks notes this as a timely warning to ensure that form and content match each other. Thus, for example, if we wish to communicate something about a historical event in biblical history, it would be unwise to choose a fable as the form in which to do it.

A third, perhaps more serious problem, about story-preaching, is discussed by Laurie Green in *Let's Do Theology* (Mowbray, London 1990). He makes the point that stories, being essentially testimonies, carry only their own intrinsic authority. We make much of listening to people's stories and taking them seriously, and we are right to do so. But stories sometimes contradict each other, are sometimes based on an inadequate understanding of life and God, and require checking from the broader Christian tradition which is scripture and history. This reinforces the importance of taking our exegetical work seriously. Only if a story is firmly based on the truth God is revealing to us in scripture, and the message it conveys is checked against our reason and the experience of the Church, is it worthy to be preached.

7 Finally

Story-sermons can be a creative and helpful way of commending the Good News, especially within the context of all-age worship. They are, of course, only *one* way of preaching, and are not in any sense intended to take the place of more traditional and conventional methods. What they have to offer is a freshness with regard to material which is over-familiar, an ability to place the hearers in a *'first-hearer'* situation, and the capacity (in the case of personalized narrative) to enable the hearers, of all ages, to make the biblical story their own story. When not over-used, they too can become part of the *'foolishness of preaching'*.

Select Bibliography and Resources

Richard A Jenson, *Telling the Story*, Augsberg Publishing House, Minneapolis USA, 1980. ISBN 0-8066-1766-7

This is the original, and so far unsurpassed, exploration of story-preaching. It is not easy reading, and does not deal specifically with all-age worship. For those who want to explore the homiletic theory involved.

Richard Coleman, *Gospel Telling*, Eerdmans, Michigan USA/Paternoster Press, Exeter 1982, ISBN 0-8028-1927-3

Sub-titled *'The art and theology of children's sermons'* this is a mixed-bag of instruction and example. Helpful on distinguishing between the various genres of story, yet still with the feel of the *'children's address'* about it.

Peter Brooks, *Communicating Conviction,* Epworth Press, London 1983. ISBN 7162-0393-6

A much under-rated book on communication, including preaching. Sections dealing specifically with story-preaching are included, but the whole book has something to offer to those who wish to communicate well to their hearers.

Kathy Galloway, *Imagining the Gospels,* SPCK, London 1988. ISBN 0-251-04388-4.

Ten *'personalized sermons'* with an introduction. Most of these are beautifully written, far too long but a real stimulus to preachers to *'have a go'*.